EVENT No. 2

CLASS "E" — NON-STOCK — 230 CUBIC INCHES AND UNDER

No.	Car	Driver	Start	Finish	Time	Place
1	Chalmers	A. E. Walden				
2	Buick	A. D. Spencer				
3	Maxwell	C. M. Hansel				
4	Ford	Guy Woodward				
5	Ford	Oily Lemon				
6	Saxon	M. A. Crocker				
7	Metz	D. W. Hickey				
8	Hispano	Jos. Boyer, Jr.			4:30	
9	Morse Cycle	E. Beeuueet			6:09	
10						

PARAMOUNT PICTURES—LYRIC THEATRE ONLY

PROGRAM

Not only in point of numbers but also in the class of the drivers, has this year's entry list for the Hill Climb been exceptional. Drivers of the caliber of Joe Dawson and Ralph De Palma are seldom seen in any events except those which are regarded as racing classics, but these famous pilots, together with many more of experience and reputation were induced to compete by the Uniontown Motoring Association through the able management of Charles W Johnson.

This is not surprising, however, as the association has from the first worked with a view toward making the Uniontown Hill Climb the classic of the U. S. in this kind of events. No other hill in the country is known to have the peculiar advantages of the Summit course and it is certain that with drivers such as have been contestants in these events, the Uniontown Hill Climb will stand in a class by itself among the hill climbing contests of the country.

Program Continued on Next Page.

2.

Uniontown Hill Climb Program 1915

© Marci Lynn McGuinness 2013

This is a reprint of the original program titled, "Program - Third Annual-Uniontown Hill Climb, June 24, 1915", donated by Gary Cooper of Charleroi, PA

ISBN: 978-0-938833-48-2

This program is part of a 4-book Uniontown Speedway set:

Yesteryear at the Uniontown Speedway
Speedway Kings of SW PA, 100 Years of Racing History
Uniontown Hill Climb (Summit Mt.) Program, 1915
Uniontown Speedway Preliminary Race Program, 1916

Order online: www.uniontownspeedway.com or www.amazon.com/author/marcimcguinness. Autographed 4-book sets: $60. (Includes S/H)

Mail orders to: Shore Publications, 145 River Street, Adah, PA 15410. Author contact: shorepublications@yahoo.com 724 710-2821

WINTON SIX

The
Nu-Size
Winton
Six
at
$2,285

Call
or
Write
for a
Demon-
stration

Allows you to select your own personal color scheme and your own guarantee.

WEST PENN AUTO COMPANY

BRACKEN C. TODD, Mgr.

Bell Phone 119-R.   BROWNSVILLE, PA.

THIRD ANNUAL SUMMIT HILL CLIMB

HELD AT

UNIONTOWN, PA., ON THE NATIONAL PIKE

FROM

HOPWOOD TO THE SUMMIT OF CHESTNUT RIDGE

A DISTANCE OF THREE MILES

THURSDAY, JUNE 24th, 1915

AT 1 P. M.

Under the rules and with the sanction of the Contest Board of the American Automobile Association, official grant No. 826, and under the rules and with the sanction of the Federation of American Motorcyclists, official sanction grant No. 2744.

Direction Of

THE UNIONTOWN MOTORING ASSOCIATION

Program Contiued on Next Page.

3.

United States
=Tire=

NOBBY TREAD
CHAIN TREAD

Mightier than the Road
Up Hill or Down Dale

Uniontown Branch
58 West Peter St.

PROGRAM—CONTINUED.

CONTEST BOARD

C. W. JOHNSON, Manager.
F A. CLOSE, Secretary.
H. D. HUTCHINSON, Treasurer.
G. B. SMITH, Advertising.
A. E. CORNS, Entries.
R. M. CAMPBELL, Reservation.
J C. SHAW, Reservation.
C. J. SMITH, Transportation.

OFFICIALS.

CHAIRMAN CONTEST BOARD—C. W. Johnson.
REFEREE—F H. Rosboro.
STARTER—A. E. Corns.
DIRECTORS OF TIMING—Wallace Miller, Ben Hunt.
DIRECTORS OF SCORING—Earl S. Areford, J Searight Marshall.
OFFICIAL REPRESENTATIVE of the A. A. A.—P D. Folwell
BOARD OF JUDGES—Webb Jay, Stewart-Warner Co., Chicago, Ill., Dale O. Pohlman, Thermoid Rubber Co., Trenton, N J.

Program Contiued on Next Page.

5.

6.

PROGRAM—CONTINUED.

TECHNICAL CHAIRMAN—John C. Donahue.
TECHNICAL COMMITTEE—John C. Donahue, James H. Mackey, Bert Abel.
FIRST ASSISTANT STARTER—G. B. Smith.
ANNOUNCING DIRECTOR—Carl Areford.
CHIEF SURGEON—Dr G. H. Robinson.
INFORMATION DIRECTOR—Ewing Marshall.
CONSULTING OFFICIALS—Hugh Chambers, E. S. Addison.

SUPERINTENDENT OF CONCESSIONS AND PROGRAM—Wendell Stone.
MANAGER OF CONCESSIONS—Ralph W Hook.
MANAGER OF PROGRAM—R. S. Reid.

RALPH DE PALMA (Mercedes) needs no introduction to race fans. De Palma won the 500 mile Indianapolis Speedway Race the 31st of last month and broke all speed records. While De Palma may not drive, we are more than glad to have him among us.

Program Continued on Next Page.

7.

8.

PROGRAM—CONTINUED.

PRIZES—AND LIST OF EVENTS.
Non-Stock—Piston Displacement (only) Classification.

EVENT No. 1—Open—Close Stripped—Stock Event. Open to Motorcycles with a piston displacement of 61.00 cubic inches and under Entry fee, $10. Prizes· First, $100; second, $75, third, $40, fourth, $25.

EVENT No. 2—Class "E," Non-Stock. Open to Class "C" cars with a piston displacement of 230 cubic inches and under Entry fee, $10. Prizes First, $100, second, $75, third, $50; fourth, $25.

EVENT No. 3—Class "D," Non-Stock, Free-for-All. Open to any gasoline car which complies with the definition of a motor car Entry fee, $50. Prizes· First, $600, second, $350, third, $250, fourth, $150, fifth, $100, sixth, $50.

NEIL WHALEN (F R. P.), is scheduled to appear but in case he is unable to whip his car into shape he will be forced to withdraw Whalen is a big leaguer and makes a specialty of dirt track racing. Few men there are who excel him at this form of contest, while in spectacularity he is second to none.

Program Continued on Next Page.

9.

10.

CROFT'S STUDIO WILL FINISH YOUR HILL CLIMB PRINTS

EVENT No. 1

MOTORCYCLES 61.00 CUBIC INCHES AND UNDER

No.	Motorcycle	Driver	Start	Finish	Time	Place
1	Excelsior	Bob Perry				
2	Excelsior	Carl Goudy			3.22	
3	Thor	W Karl Benz				
4	Indian					
5	Indian					
6	Merkle	Maldwyn Jones				
7	Harley-Davison					
8	Harley-Davison				3.13	
9						
10						
11						
12						
13						
14						
15						

SEE "THE ABSENTEE" AT THE LYRIC TODAY.

11.

PROGRAM—CONTINUED.

HOW THE RACE IS RUN

A Concise Account of How the Big Event Is Managed.

SANCTION—The third annual Hill Climb, like all preceding contests of its type, is run under the supervision of the American Automobile Association, the governing body of the sport. An official representative of the organization is in supreme control, with a referee as his chief executive and two assistants, in the roles of starter and chairman of the technical committee, respectively. Minor appointments are made with the sanction of these officials.

JUDGES—Order of the finish, in the event of a close race, is decided by the Judges, while cases of unfair driving are passed on by umpires, stationed at regular intervals on the course.

ELIGIBILITY—All drivers must be registered with the contest board of the American Automobile Association and hold registry cards issued by the contest board. Their cars are inspected by the technical committee to see that they comply with the contest rules.

START—A flying start of 100 yards is given all the contestants in each event. As the starter's flag drops, the car is under way.

TIMING—Timing is by electricity. The Hill Climb instrument being invented by Mr. A. M. Crichton, of the Tri-State Telegraph & Telephone Co., and being so accurate as to register a fraction of a second. Almost immediately information of results is available.

SCORING—The official score is kept by hand, no instrument having been invented as yet quite as reliable as the old-fashioned way.

Program Contiued on Next Page

13.

PROGRAM—CONTINUED.

ANNOUNCING—Information as to the progress of the race is transmitted to the spectators by means of telephones and announcers stationed at the start, Turkey's Nest, Watering Trough, Point Look Out and Summit.

SIGNAL FLAGS—Signal flags generally used during a contest of this kind are red, yellow and blue. The red flag indicating a clear course, the yellow flag meaning to stop immediately, the blue flag indicating that there has been an accident on the course. These flags are for signaling the racing cars only

POLICE—Provisions for safety of spectators are most complete, a thoroughly competent organization of guards handling every detail of the policing, together with numerous detectives and special officers. Spectators are warned to be on their guard against theft or fraud.

HOSPITAL—A hospital tent will be erected at the Turkey's Nest, in charge of Dr. G. H. Robinson, to take care of contestants, whether injured or overcome by the strain. Dr. Robinson will be assisted by the First Aid Team of the Oliver-Snyder plant.

ADMINISTRATION—In general, the facilities built up by the Hill Climb management for the conduct of a race are about as complete as possible, three years of experience having done wonders towards systematization. Each year teaches new lessons, requiring further changes. Eventually it is hoped to approximate perfection as closely as it is possible for human beings to do. In the meanwhile, the management craves the kind indulgence of its patrons for any slight aberrations that might occur.

Program Continued on Next Page.

NATIONAL AUTO COMPANY

64-70 West Fayette Street

The Home of the

Hudson, Overland and

Marmon

ATLANTIC GASOLENE AND OILS

16.

PROGRAM—CONTINUED

JOE DAWSON (Marmon). The youthful winner of the 1912 Indianapolis 500 mile race was scheduled to appear here last year but was confined to the hospital at the time as the result of serious injuries received at Indianapolis several weeks previous.

Dawson has a racing career second to none. Starting as a Marmon tester, he plunged to the front in daredevil fashion, always speeding as fast as his machine would go. Despite his tendency to "step on it," however, Dawson has always displayed the coolest of judgment under fire. A better judge of pace and position never lived. Knowing to a fraction of a second what his mount is capable of, he invariably drives it to the limit of safety and holds it there. If he fails to win, it is usually due to some other reason than lack of personal ability

What he is able to do with his Marmon in the way of hill climbing, we have yet to discover

I. P FETTERMAN (Simplex), well-known to the local people by reason of his dare-devil driving last year, has made up his mind that his luck in hill climbing will change some day, and that, accordingly, he will keep on trying. Fetterman has confined his racing chiefly to this section of Pennsylvania and Ohio in the last year and consequently he will have many friends present.

Program Continued on Next Page.

17.

Correct Lubrication

Explanation: In the Chart below, the letter opposite the car indicates the grade of Gargoyle Mobiloils that should be used. For example, "A" means Gargoyle Mobiloil "A", "Arc" means Gargoyle Mobiloil "Arctic." The recommendations cover all models of both pleasure and commercial vehicles unless otherwise noted.

MODEL OF CARS	1911 Summer	1911 Winter	1912 Summer	1912 Winter	1913 Summer	1913 Winter	1914 Summer	1914 Winter	1915 Summer	1915 Winter
Abbott Detroit	A	Arc	A	Arc	A	Arc	A	Arc	A	Arc

Oil Wear

How often do you stop for oil?

DO you watch to see whether your oil "wears" well or poorly?

You should.

You may be sure of this: An oil that "wears" poorly lubricates poorly.

For the next 500 miles note down the quantity of oil you use.

Then clean out your motor. For the following 500 miles use the grade of Gargoyle Mobiloils specified for your car in the Chart on this page. Again note the quantity consumed.

The result will demonstrate the superior "wear" of the correct grade of Gargoyle Mobiloils. To many motorists the difference is astonishing.

Mobiloils

A grade for each type of motor

What accounts for it?

It is due partly to the oil's *lubricating efficiency*—which remains unimpaired under the heat of service—and partly to the correctness of the oil's *body*, which assures an adequate supply to all working parts and a perfect seal between pistons and cylinder walls.

With a perfect piston seal, fuel gases cannot blow past the piston rings, destroying the oil film, and wasting power; nor can undue quantities of oil work into the combustion chambers and form troublesome carbon deposits.

The "wear" of the grade of Gargoyle Mobiloils specified for your car will give you striking proof of its lubricating efficiency.

At the left we print in part our Chart of Automobile Recommendations. For a number of years, this Chart which represents our professional advice has been the motorist's standard guide to scientifically-correct lubrication.

If your car does not appear in the partial Chart on this page, we will gladly mail you a complete Chart on request.

VACUUM OIL COMPANY
Rochester, N. Y., U. S. A.

Specialists in the manufacture of high-grade lubricants for every class of machinery. Obtainable everywhere in the world.

Domestic Branches:	Detroit Pittsburgh	Boston Philadelphia	New York Indianapolis	Chicago Minneapolis

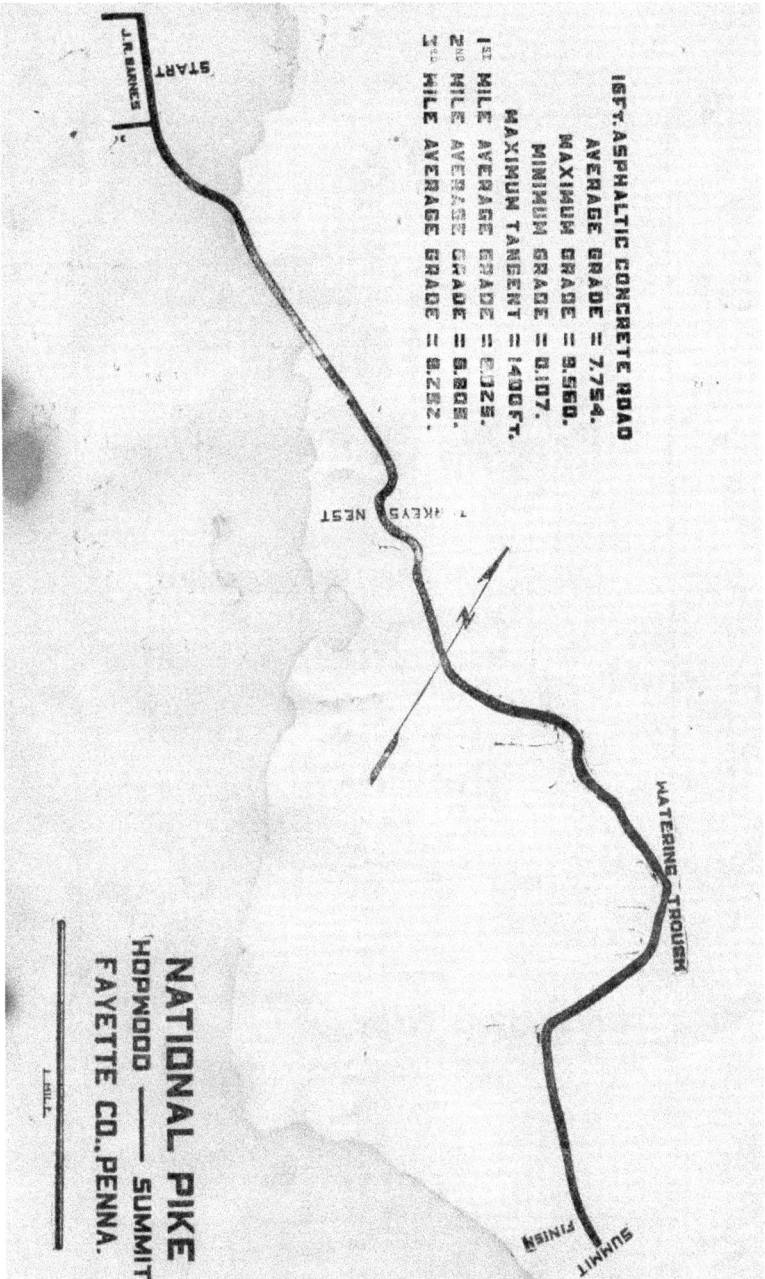

START
J.R.BARNES

1 FT. ASPHALTIC CONCRETE ROAD
AVERAGE GRADE = 7.754.
MAXIMUM GRADE = 9.560.
MINIMUM GRADE = 0.107.
MAXIMUM TANGENT = 1400 FT.
1ST MILE AVERAGE GRADE = 8.025.
2ND MILE AVERAGE GRADE = 8.905.
3RD MILE AVERAGE GRADE = 8.282.

TURKEYS NEST

WATERING TROUGH

SUMMIT
FINISH

NATIONAL PIKE
HOPWOOD — SUMMIT
FAYETTE CO. PENNA.

1 MILE

BOTH PHONES

480

Cars for All Occasions

CALL US FOR PRICES ON OUR 15 PAS-
SENGER CAR FOR PICNICS, WED-
DINGS, FUNERALS, Etc.

Our Prices Are Reasonable

CITY TAXI RATES, 25 CENTS

Uniontown Taxicab Co.

BROADWAY

C. J. SMITH, Manager.

20.

PROGRAM—CONTINUED.

C. W. JOHNSON (Buick), the pioneer automobile man of Uniontown occupies a niche in the hearts of the local public that no one else can fill. Johnson burst into prominence through his Uniontown-Philadelphia road race and last year's Hill Climb. What "Charlie" does not know about the National Pike between Hopwood and the Summit is not worth printing. Outside of racing events, Johnson has been known to shoot his car up the tortuous mountain incline many seconds faster than the record holders. "Charlie" will also drive a Packard.

C. M. WILLIAMS (Darracq), conclusively demonstrated his real ability in the last Hill Climb, by finishing third, being beaten out of second place by less than half a second. Williams figures that as his French car was able to take first money at Palm Beach under the guidance of "The Flying Dutchman," there is more than a good showing awaiting it at the Summit.

H. E. CUPPS (Lozier), has made a specialty of dirt track racing. His entrance is due to Dr Chambers of McKeesport who has a reputation of being an expert judge of drivers. The coming races will show whether Chamber's judgment is correct.

Program Continued on Next Page.

21.

PROGRAM—CONTINUED.

JOSEPH W DICKINSON (Stutz) claims New Jersey as his home, and has figured in dirt track meets and hill climbs throughout the east for a number of years. Dickinson is campaigning with a Stutz and is said to have negotiated an especially difficult grade at Norristown, Pa., at a phenominal speed. In all of his activities there is present a grim resolve to make good. Once he has his mind made up, nothing short of an earthquake can move him.

JOSEPH BOYCE, JR., (Hispanosuiza), of Cleveland, claims that the foreign car from the sunny climes of Italy will far surpass anything in the way of hill climbing to be seen. There has been a great deal of press comment about this Italian racer which is commonly known to the American public as the "Hispano," and it is our wish that its climb for fame will not be hindered by its showing in the present races.

ROY STENTZ (Buick) has agreed to drive the "Yellow Kid" for "Charlie" Johnson in order that the latter may be able to devote his time entirely to his Packard "Greyhound." Stentz is quite a local favorite, having been in the automobile business from infancy Considered the best mechanic in the county and with all the nerve and skill required of a driver, it is expected that he will be one of the first money takers.

Program Continued on Next Page.

TRI-STATE GARAGE CO.

70-74 E. FAYETTE STREET

The Garage that repairs your car—

The Garage that is equipped for repairing cars—

The Garage that repairs any car—

The Service Station for Studebaker Cars—

The Service for Ford Cars with all parts carried in stock in quantities.

A fine line of accessories of best quality.

Prompt service, Courteous treatment and a Square Deal.

Come and see us when in need of our services.

R. M. CAMPBELL

PROPRIETOR

24.

PROGRAM—CONTINUED.

JOSEPH RYAN (Mercer), hails from New York State. His previous experience consists chiefly in breaking the speed laws of New York and lowering the inter-city records of the state. He as figured in numerous small dirt track races and now has the desire to add some Hill climbing trophies to his list.

BILL POFFENBERGER (Marmon), also a big figure in the races last year, is back again for another trial at the most difficult of all motor sports, hill climbing. This year Poffenberger is expected to prove a sensation. This is said to be due to the experience he has acquired of late. Nor has he much in the way of victories to enthuse about since they have been few and far between. True, he has cleand up in a number of small dirt track meets, but to one of larger achievement, this is but small comfort.

F J SWARTZENBERGER (Duesenberg), who made such a remarkable showing last year in practice and who unfortunately burned a bearing out of his car the morning of the race, will be on hand. This year F J brings a different car which he claims will far surpass his try-outs of the previous season. We hope that no unfortunate circumstances will keep this speed king out of the money in the present races.

Program Contiued on Next Page.

26

PROGRAM—CONTINUED.

BOB PERRY (Excelsior) holds a seat on the Excelsior Team and is an adventurer born and bred, a man who has knocked about from one corner of the globe to the other. Although motorcycle racing is now a past sport, it is safe to say that were it still in vogue, Perry's name would be found at the head of the list.

DICK GOUDY (Excelsior), a team-mate of Perry, has really not been in the game long enough to give an adequate demonstration of his ability but the fact that he comes from the Excelsior factory in such company is a sure sign he has the requirements of a winner. We might add that it was through the team work of Goudy that Bob Perry won the Milwaukee Race last Saturday

D. W. HICKEY (Metz) is one of the favorite entries in the second race. His favoritism is due somewhat to the fact that a Metz won last year's race. We know little of the ability of this youngster but coming from Masontown is a great asset.

Program Continued on Next Page.

27.

FORD
FORD
FORD
FORD
FORD

FORD

FORD

FORD

SHAW MOTOR COMPANY
South Gallatin Avenue

28.

Two of the Mercer Entries Trying Out on the Pike.

IF YOU WANT TO GO THE BEST WAY
—USE THE—
Union Pacific Railroad
The Most Direct and Scenic Route to

DENVER   SEATTLE
SALT LAKE CITY   SPOKANE
   YELLOWSTONE PARK   SAN DIEGO
   PORTLAND   LOS ANGELES
        SAN FRANCISCO

The only double track electric block system road West of the Missouri River, and 10 through trains daily including America's foremost De Luxe Train, "The Overland Limited," Chicago to the Pacific Coast.

Tell your local ticket agent to have your ticket read over this route and for further information and literature, write

J. E. CORFIELD,
GENERAL AGENT,
539 Smithfield Street,   PITTSBURGH, PA.

29.

www.uniontownspeedway.com

PROGRAM—CONTINUED.

A. D. SPENCER (Buick), of Charleroi, is making his real Hill Climb debut with his string of racers. Spencer's bravery and daring, and above all, his sensational exploits of racing recklessness, have surrounded him with a halo shared by few other drivers.

MADLWYN JONES (Merkle) is one of the big favorites in the motorcycle race. Jones comes from the state where most cycle riders originate, making his headquarters at Lebanon, Ohio. Wherever there is a motorcycle meet you will find Jones.

JAMES BENEDICT (Isotta) was one of the big figures in the Hill Climb last year, but a streak of hard luck kept him out of the money. Benedict is a very quiet fellow and when he said last year that he would be back "with a car that will clean up,' we believed he would keep his word, and, at least, he is here. Hailing from New York City, Benedict has won quite a few races at Brighton Beach.

ALVA HUGHSON—F M. SEANOR (Haynes) represent a fast aggregation from the Pittsburgh Branch of the Haynes Automobile Company

A. PHERSON (Mercer) is there with any of them when it comes to climbing hills. He drives for I. Ambler

Program Continued on Next Page.

31.

PACKARD FRANKLIN
CHANDLER
BUICK DODGE BROS.

When Better Automobiles Are Sold We Will Sell Them.

STANDARD
AUTOMOBILE GARAGE

ARCH AND PETER STREETS

UNIONTOWN, PA.

$25,000 STOCK OF ACCESSORIES

32.

PROGRAM—CONTINUED.

BEN HILL (Fiat), is one of the most popular eastern drivers, having made a name for himself throughout the New England states and on the Atlantic coast as one of the most fearless drivers in the race game today The fact that he makes his headquarters in Brooklyn as well as his savake style of driving, has caused Ben Hill to be dubbed the terror of the Coney Island Boulevard. Hill owes his opportunity to the support of Al. Broderick, a Brooklyn race promoter with a craving for speed, more speed, and still more speed.

FRED CLOSE (Chalmers) was the first driver and we hope the last to meet with an accident this year. While testing out his car last Saturday, Close ran into the ditch and hit a telephone pole, snapping it off short. The car which was considerably damaged has been repaired, but a driver from the Chalmers' factory is expected to take the place of Close who was slightly injured about the back.

Program Contiued on Next Page.

THERE IS MORE POWER
IN THAT

GOOD GULF GASOLINE

A Clean, Powerful Gasoline refined
especially for the automobile trade

and

SUPREME AUTO OIL

THE PERFECT LUBRICANT

GULF REFINING COMPANY

PITTSBURGH, PA.

General Sales Ofices
The Largest Independent Refininig Company
in the World.

TOURING MAPS may be obtained from any
dealer displaying the orange disc sign—
or mailed on request.

34.

HAROLD LOCKWOOD AT THE LYRIC SATURDAY.

PROGRAM—CONTINUED.

T S. O'RORKE (Overland) has been handling a steering wheel ever since he was fourteen years old. A careful analysis of O'Rorke racing proves him of the most methodical sort but with absolute fearlessness.

T. P ROSE (Mercedes) is a team mate of Fetterman and drives with the same spectacularity. These two veterans with a Simplex and a Mercedes form the racing squad of A. C. Smith.

G. B. GARDNER (Beaver Bullet) was Charles King's mechanician in the 1914 Indianapolis race in which the Bullet was the second American car to finish. On his second trial over the local course Tuesday, Gardner made it in 3:58.

Program Continued on Next Page.

35.

CROFT'S STUDIO WILL FINISH YOUR HILL CLIMB FILMS

EVENT No. 3

CLASS "D" — NON-STOCK — FREE-FOR-ALL

No.	Car	Driver	Start	Finish	Time	Place
1	Overland	T. S. O'Rorke			6 13	
2	Dickinson Special	J. W. Dickinson			3 54	
3	Hispano Suiza	Jos. Boyer, Jr				
4	Isotta	Jas. Benedict				
5	Simplex	I. P. Fetterman			3 46	
6	Beaver Bullet	G. B. Gardner				
7	Darracq Special	C. M. Williams				
8	Buick 16	Roy Stentz			4 10	
9	Haynes	Alva Hughson				
10	Mercer	Jos. J. Ryan				
11	Mercedes	T. P. Rose				
12	Mercer	A. Pherson				
13	Packard	C. W. Johnson			3 27	
14	Lozier	H. E. Cupps				
15	Fiat Special	Ben Hill				
16	Chalmers	A. E. Walden			3 48	
17	Haynes	F. M. Seanor				
18	Buick	A. D. Spencer				
19	Marmon	Joe Dawson			3 47	
20	Mercedes Special	Ralph De Palma			3 33	
21						

VISIT THE LYRIC AFTER THE RACES

36.

Marci Lynn McGuinness
History of Summit Mountain Hill Climbs
1913 - 1916

The first Summit Mountain Hill Climb was organized by George Flavious Titlow and his Fayette County Automobile Club in 1913. The first year was amateur and held on the east side of the mountain. In 1914, a professional race was held on the west side from Hopwood to the top of the Summit at the Summit Hotel. Motorcycles also competed. Firestone Tires sponsored the race that attracted 4,000 spectators.

In 1915, after Ralph DePalma won the Indianapolis 500, he was beat at the Summit Mountain Hill Climb by Uniontown's Charlie Johnson before 25,000 race fans lining the mountainsides.

As the fourth annual hill climb was being planned, the Department of Transportation outlawed the hill climbs. This prompted Johnson, Titlow and coal barons to build the 1 1/8th mile oval Uniontown Speedway board track. It was internationally famous for seven years with Tommy Milton and Jimmy Murphy setting 52 AAA speed records in Duesenbergs in 1919 here. These records held through the mid 1960's.

Author Marci Lynn McGuinness has reprinted this program for your enjoyment. It is part of her 4-book speedway series.

Yesteryear at the Uniontown Speedway
Speedway Kings of SW PA, 100 Years of Racing History
Uniontown Hill Climb (Summit Mt.) Program, 1915
Uniontown Speedway Preliminary Race Program, 1916
PLUS: Speedway Kings – The Video
Speed Kings, the screenplay, is seeking a film producer.

Uniontown Hill Climb Program 1915

Celebrate the 100 Year Anniversary of the 1913 Summit Mountain Hill Climb.
Joe Boyer in his Hispana Suiza #3, June 24, 1915 - the last hill climb.

Vintage auto enthusiasts & race history fans are cordially invited to celebrate a century of racing, June 14 & 15, 2014.

Join Marci McGuinness, the National Road Heritage Corridor, the Summit Inn and National Road businesses on a two-day Father's Day weekend celebration of the automobile. Tour National Road sites on Saturday. Climb Summit Mt. Sunday. Car show, presentations and festival at the Summit Inn below the pool area, Sunday, 10 a. m. - 3 p. m.

Great Father's Day FUN for Father/Son teams to drive their old cars and motorcycles up Summit Mountain. Do it for Dad. MAKE HIS DAY!
Call: 724 710-2821

Dave Dahl pictured above, Summit Mountain Hill Climb 2013

Your Banking

Why not make this bank your place of Deposit. We are equipped to serve you in every way it is possible for a bank to serve.

Capital	Total
$150,000	Resources
Surplus	Over
$320,000	$2,300,000

Business and Personal Checking Accounts Receive Close Attention.

4% INTEREST PAID ON SAVINGS ACCOUNTS.

Citizens Title & Trust Company

www.ingramcontent.com/pod-product-compliance
Lightning Source LLC
Chambersburg PA
CBHW071751020426
42331CB00008B/2274